A New True Book

LAOS

By Karen Jacobsen

CHILDRENS PRESS®
CHICAGO

On a rainy day, a Laotian girl stays dry under a huge banana leaf.

PHOTO CREDITS

AP/Wide World Photos—7, 26 (2 photos), 29, 31, 32

Reprinted with permission of *The New Book of Knowledge*, 1989 edition, © Grolier Inc.—5

Historical Pictures Service—22

Journalism Services—© P. Benaich, 9 (left), 18, 38 (right)

North Wind Picture Archives—23

PhotoEdit—© Mark Richards, 34 (left)

Photri—Cover Inset, 6, 8 (top right), 9 (right), 13 (left), 15 (right), 34 (right), 35, 38 (left), 39 (2 photos)

© Carl Purcell—2, 11 (left), 13 (right), 15 (left), 16, 19, 36, 40 (center and right), 45 (3 photos)

Shostal Associates/SuperStock International, Inc.—8 (top left and bottom right), 20

The Stock Market—© Bruce Thomas, 17 (left), 24, 44

SuperStock International, Inc.—© S. Rostas, Cover; © Baldev, 11 (center); © Roger Bardot, 42 (2 photos)

Third Coast Stock Source—© Michael Douglas, 17 (right)

TSW-CLICK/Chicago—© Mary Wolf, 40 (left); © Chad Slattery, 44 (inset)

UPI/Bettmann Newsphotos—41

Valan—© Paul L. Janosi, 11 (right)

COVER: Nam Khan River, Luang Prabang, Laos

COVER INSET: Young woman and child of the ancient Yao tribe

Library of Congress Cataloging-in-Publication Data

Jacobsen, Karen.
Laos / by Karen Jacobsen.
p. cm. — (A New true book)
Includes index.
Summary: An introduction to the only landlocked occupant of the Indochinese peninsula.
ISBN 0-516-01113-8
1. Laos—Juvenile literature. [1. Laos.] I. Title.
DS555.3.J33 1991 90-21034
959.4—dc20 CIP
AC

Printed in the United States of America.
1 2 3 4 5 6 7 8 9 10 R 00 99 98 97 96 95 94 93 92 91

TABLE OF CONTENTS

THE LAND

Laos is a long and narrow country in Southeast Asia. Laos has no seacoast. It is surrounded by five other countries—Thailand, Burma (Myanmar), China, Vietnam, and Cambodia.

In parts of Laos, monsoons drop more than 100 inches of rain each year. During July and August, the rain falls for days without stopping, and the

Laos is part of a large peninsula called Indochina.

temperatures are very warm. But, from January through April, there is not much rainfall, and the temperatures become a little cooler.

In northern Laos, rugged mountains are broken by valleys.

Mountains and steep valleys cover northern Laos. In northeastern Laos there is a hilly, grass-covered plateau called the Plain of Jars. More than one hundred

Today, some people think the jars found in the Plain of Jars held grain or liquor. Others think they were used to bury the dead. But no one knows for sure.

large stone jars are spread over the plain. The jars are a mystery. They were made long before people kept written records.

The Mekong River flows south from China through

Rice is grown in flooded fields called paddies (right). Boats carry fresh food and other products to market towns up and down the Mekong River (above and top right).

Laos. Its waters irrigate rice paddies and carry boat traffic.

The largest towns and cities in Laos are on or near

Left: A street in Vientiane.
Above: A village on the Mekong River in northern Laos.

the Mekong River. Luang Prabang, in the center of northern Laos, is the country's ancient capital. Farther downriver is Vientiane, the new capital and the largest city in Laos.

The Annamese mountain chain forms a natural border between eastern Laos and Vietnam.

The Bolovens Plateau lies in southern Laos, between the Annamese Mountains and the Mekong River. Many crops are grown here.

Almost two-thirds of Laos is covered with forests. Many wild animals live in the mountains, jungles, and rivers of Laos. There are leopards, tigers, wild buffalo,

Crocodiles (above left), monkeys (left), and leopards (above) make their homes in the forests and rivers of Laos.

monkeys, crocodiles, and many more.

The largest animal is the elephant. Long ago, Laos was known as the Land of a Million Elephants. But today, there are not many elephants left.

THE NATION

The official name of Laos is the Lao People's Democratic Republic. For more than fifteen hundred years, Laos was a kingdom. Then, in 1975, the last king gave up his throne, and Laos became a republic. Laos is a socialist country. Its people share in owning all of the property in their country. The Laotian Communist Party makes the laws and runs the government.

Buddhist monks (left) live simple lives. A Laotian child (right)

THE PEOPLE

There are about four million people in Laos. They belong to more than sixty different tribes. Each tribe has its own language and customs. There are three main groups: the Lao Lum, the Lao Theung, and the Lao Suong.

Half of the people in Laos are Lao Lum. They grow rice in the lowland river valleys.

Lao Lum men plow the fields, make tools and canoes, build houses, hunt, and trade. The women plant and harvest the rice, grow the vegetables, tend to the animals, cook the meals, weave cloth, and sew the family's clothes.

The Lao Lum are Buddhists. Almost every

Lao Lum houses stand on poles and are built of bamboo and rattan. The rooms are open and airy.

village has a Buddhist temple, called a wat.

The Lao Theung lived in Laos before the Lao Lum. But, long ago, the Lao Lum invaded the country and made slaves of the Lao Theung. Even in modern times, the Lao Theung were treated badly by the Lao Lum. But now the Lao Theung have equal rights.

The Lao Theung are farmers. They keep water buffalo as work animals. They raise pigs and chickens for food.

Water buffalos are tame animals. They are strong enough to pull a plow through the heavy mud of the flooded rice paddies.

A woman (above) carries water for crops. A young girl (right) shows off her colorful Hmong clothing.

The Lao Suong are made up of several tribes of people, such as the Hmong, the Mien, and the Man. They live in villages near the tops of the mountains. They raise animals and small crops of rice and corn.

When there is work to be done, family members work together.

Most people in Laos work and live on farms. Only fifteen percent of the people work and live in cities or towns.

Most of the buildings in Laotian cities are new. The old buildings and roads were destroyed by bombs in the wars of the 1960s and 1970s.

There are not many trucks or automobiles in Laos. Most of the roads are only dirt trails.

During the rainy season, many dirt roads become almost impossible to use.

Laos is a very poor country. It has few products and industries. But Laos has deposits of tin, iron, zinc, gold, silver, and other minerals. Its government is working to develop ways to use these resources.

A brick factory

LAOS LONG AGO

About 1,200 years ago, the Tai people moved south from China into present-day Laos and Thailand. Tai warriors drove the Lao Theung people living in the river valleys away. Today, in Laos, the Tai are known as Lao Lum.

The most famous king in Laotian history is Fa Ngoun (1316-1373). He had wealth and great power. His kingdom was called Lan

This drawing shows the royal elephant—the symbol of the kingdom of Lan Xang.

Xang, the Land of a Million Elephants. Fa Ngoun made Buddhism the religion of Lan Xang.

By 1717, Lan Xang had broken into four small, weak kingdoms: Luang Prabang, Vientiane, Champassak, and Xieng Khouang.

FRANCE AND INDOCHINA

In 1865, traders from France came to Southeast Asia. They wanted to start a French colony. By 1893, the French had taken over all of the Laotian kingdoms. Then, in 1899, the French joined

French soldiers capture a Laotian village.

This palace in Luang Prabang was built by the French in the nineteenth century.

them into one colony named Laos. The French chose the king of Luang Prabang to be the king of Laos. But he had little power and obeyed French orders.

France also ruled in Vietnam and Cambodia.

Together, the three colonies were called French Indochina.

In 1941, during World War II, the Japanese captured French Indochina. After Japan was defeated in 1945, King Sisouvang Vong of Luang Prabang and three of his sons—Phetsarath, Souvanna Phouma, and Souphanouvong—took power in Laos.

But the French came back. Their army defeated the Laotian army. By April

Prince Souphanouvong and his wife (above) and Prince Souvanna Phouma (right)

1946, the king and his family had fled to Thailand. France again ruled Laos.

In 1949, Souvanna Phouma returned to Laos. He was made premier in the new government. His brother, Souphanouvong, didn't trust the French. He joined the Pathet Lao, a group of Laotian Communists. The Pathet Lao wanted the French out of Laos.

In Vietnam, the French were fighting an army of Vietnamese Communists, led by Ho Chi Minh. In 1954, the Communists defeated the French at the battle of Dien Bien Phu.

At a peace conference in Geneva, Switzerland, the French gave up French Indochina. Vietnam was divided into two parts—North Vietnam and South Vietnam. Laos was made into a neutral country.

Again, Souvanna Phouma became the head of the government. Souphanouvong returned to Laos. In 1958, a new National Assembly was elected.

THE STRUGGLE FOR POWER

In 1960, Captain Kong Le took control of the army and overthrew the government. Kong Le wanted a neutral government for Laos—not Communist and not military.

Captain Kong Le was from the Lao Theung hill tribes. He wanted the Laotians to stop fighting each other.

He made Souvanna Phouma the premier of his government.

Soon, there were three groups fighting to control Laos—the old military leaders, Kong Le's army, and the Pathet Lao, led by Souphanouvong.

To end the fighting, there was a second Geneva Conference in 1962. Again, the world powers agreed to make Laos neutral, with a government made up of representatives from all

Boun Oum, Souvanna Phouma, and Souphanouvong
(left to right) sign an agreement.

three groups. Souvanna Phouma, Souphanouvong, and Prince Boun Oum (of the Champassak royal family) led the new government.

But Souphanouvong quit the government in 1963 and rejoined the Pathet Lao to fight for a Communist Laos.

The Pathet Lao were a powerful, disciplined group.

Beginning in 1961, thousands of United States troops joined with South Vietnam to fight the Vietnamese Communists. The United States also had thousands of troops in Laos. In 1973, the United States stopped fighting and the American troops left Vietnam and Laos. By 1975, the Communists had taken over all of Vietnam. In Laos, the Pathet Lao formed a Communist government. Souphanouvong was its president, and Kaysone Phoumvihan became its prime minister. Souvanna Phouma was an adviser.

Kaysone Phoumvihan and the Communist government took over all the wealth and property in the country.

Children are cared for by all members of the family (left).
Laotians at an open-air market (right)

Laos is poor. Most people have some food, a place to live, and basic clothing. But there is hunger and disease.

The government is trying to make life better. But it has very little money, and making changes is expensive.

Some parts of Laos still have no school buildings or classes for students. There are not enough teachers or books in any school.

EDUCATION

The government supports education. In the towns and cities, there are five-year primary schools and six-year secondary schools. All of the classes are free and are

In many places Buddhist monks run classes for male students.

taught in the Lao language. Students learn basic subjects and work in teams to improve their grades.

More males than females have the chance to go to school.

Laos has some special schools for training teachers and for teaching agricultural and technical subjects. Advanced students study law, medicine, and government at Sisavongvong University in Vientiane.

Finely carved doors (left) on a Buddhist temple. The That Luang (above) is a Buddhist shrine in Vientiane.

ARTS AND CRAFTS

Most of old Laos was destroyed during the country's many wars. But, some examples of ancient arts still remain. In the wats, there are finely carved wooden doors, pulpits, and chests.

Stone and bronze statues of Buddha are seen everywhere in Laos. The silverwork of Laotian

A sleeping Buddha carved in stone (left). A sitting Buddha (right) greets visitors to a temple in Luang Prabang.

Coins that decorate clothing (left), a bracelet (above), and a necklace (right) are examples of Laotian silverwork.

jewelers is valued at home and around the world. Silkweaving with gold or silver threads is an advanced craft in Laos.

Laotian people enjoy plays with characters that tease each other or

A musician plays a traditional bamboo instrument.

exchange insults. Musical plays are also favorites.

The lamvong is a favorite dance for couples in Laos. Music is played on cymbals, strings, a xylophone, and the khene—a Laotian flute made from many lengths of bamboo.

This family works together in a tailor shop (above). When work is done, Laotians enjoy watching soccer matches (below).

SPORTS AND GAMES

Laotians have to work hard to make a living. But they do take time for fun. Young children play with simple handmade toys.

The favorite sport is soccer. When young people play soccer, everyone likes to watch.

The Mekong River winds past the farmlands and cities of Laos. Buddhist temples (inset) are everywhere in the land.

The many peoples of Laos are learning to live together in peace.

The Lao live simply. Family members depend on each other for help. At last, there is peace in Laos. Will the Communist government give Laotians freedom? Only time will tell.

WORDS YOU SHOULD KNOW

ancient (AIN • shent)—of very great age; from a long time ago
border (BORE • der)—edge, boundary
capital (KAP • ih • til)—city where a country's government in located
colony (KAH • luh • nee)—a settlement of people from another country or place
Communist (KAHM • yoo • nist)—a person who believes in a system of government under which businesses are owned by the state
crop (CRAHP)—plants grown to be used as food
government (GUV • ern • ment)—a system of ruling a city, state, or country
Indochina (in • doh • CHY • nah)—a large peninsula east of India and south of China
irrigate (EER • ih • gate)—to supply water by a pipe or ditch system
khene (HEEN)—a Laotian flute made with several bamboo tubes
lamvong (LAHM • vong)—a Laotian dance
Lao Lum (LAH • oh LUHM)—Laotians of the valleys; they came from China long ago
Lao Suong (LAH • oh soo • ONG)—Laotians of the mountaintops; there are many different Lao Suong tribes
Lao Theung (LAH • oh THAY • ung)—Laotians of the mountainsides; descendants of the first people of Laos; made into slaves by the first Lao Lum settlers from China.
monsoon (mahn • SOON)—a strong wind in southern Asia; often blows heavy rains from the ocean onto the mainland
neutral (NOO • tril)—taking neither side; not involved